Count Your Way through

Israel

by Jim Haskins

illustrations by Rick Hanson

 Carolrhoda Books, Inc./Minneapolis

Special thanks to Steffi Karen Rubin.

This edition of this book is available in two bindings:
Library binding by Carolrhoda Books, Inc.
Soft cover by First Avenue Editions
241 First Avenue North
Minneapolis, MN 55401

LIBRARY OF CONGRESS CATALOGING-IN-PUBLICATION DATA

Haskins, James, 1941-
    Count your way through Israel / by Jim Haskins; illustrations by Rick Hanson.
        p.   cm.
    Summary: An introduction to the land and people of Israel accompanied by instructions on how to read and pronounce the numbers one through ten in Hebrew.
    ISBN 0-87614-415-6 (lib. bdg.)
    ISBN 0-87614-558-6 (pbk.)
    1. Israel—Juvenile literature. 2. Counting—Juvenile literature. [1. Israel. 2. Counting.] I. Hanson, Rick, ill.
II. Title.
DS102.95.H37   1990
954—dc20
[E]   90-1594
                                                          CIP
                                                           AC

Manufactured in the United States of America

    2 3 4 5 6 7 8 9 10 99 98 97 96 95 94 93 92 91

In Hebrew, the first ten letters of the alphabet are used for the numerals 1-10. For example, the second letter of the alphabet is used to represent the number 2. As you count your way through Israel in Hebrew, you will find the corresponding letter/numerals integrated into the borders of the art.

Introductory Note

Since ancient times, the Hebrew language has been spoken by people of the Jewish faith. Traditionally, the Jewish people lived in the land that is now Israel. But at different times in history, they were driven out of the area by conquering nations.

In 1948, the United Nations established the State of Israel as a Jewish homeland. Hebrew became one of Israel's two official languages.

Israel's second official language is Arabic. Israel is located in what was once Palestine. When the State of Israel was founded, war broke out between the Jewish settlers and the Arabs who lived in the region. The war caused large numbers of Palestinians to flee. But many stayed, and they make up a sizable portion of Israel's population.

In this book, we will count our way through Israel in Hebrew. Hebrew is written from right to left. The alphabet has 26 characters, all consonants. When vowel sounds are needed, vowel symbols are placed above, below, or to the side of the consonants. (Some consonants are also used as vowels.)

Many of the sounds used in Hebrew are different from those of English. Hebrew has two *h* sounds. One is like the English *h*. The other *h* sounds like a combination of a *k* and an *h*. This sound is represented by a capital *H* in the pronunciation guides.

1

אחת (ah-Hat)

Israel is a land of diverse cultures. It is **one** country in the land bridge between Africa (to the west) and Asia and Europe (to the east and north). Because of its location, the area now called Israel has long been a crossroads of the Middle East, important for trade and conquest. Over the centuries, this land has been ruled by many different peoples and nations. Since Israel became a state, Jewish people from almost every continent of the world have come to live there.

AFRICA

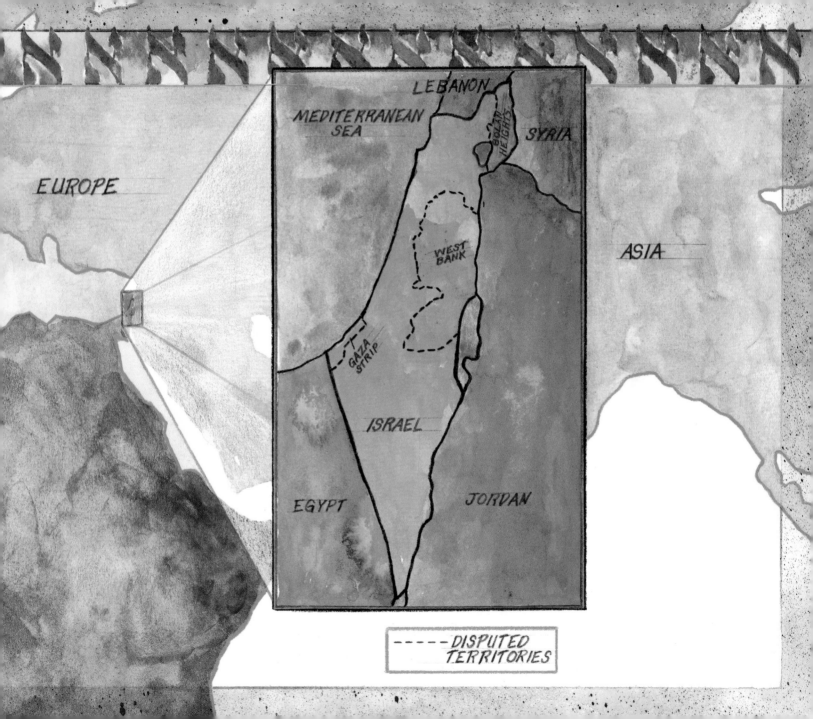

2

שתים (shtah-yim)

In the biblical story of **two** men, David and Goliath, the shepherd David must fight against the giant Goliath. David manages to win by using his wits and a slingshot. Because Israel is surrounded by Arab countries, many Jewish Israelis feel that they are like David facing Goliath. They believe that they must fight, using their wits, to survive in the Middle East. Since Israel's founding, the country has been in many struggles with neighboring countries.

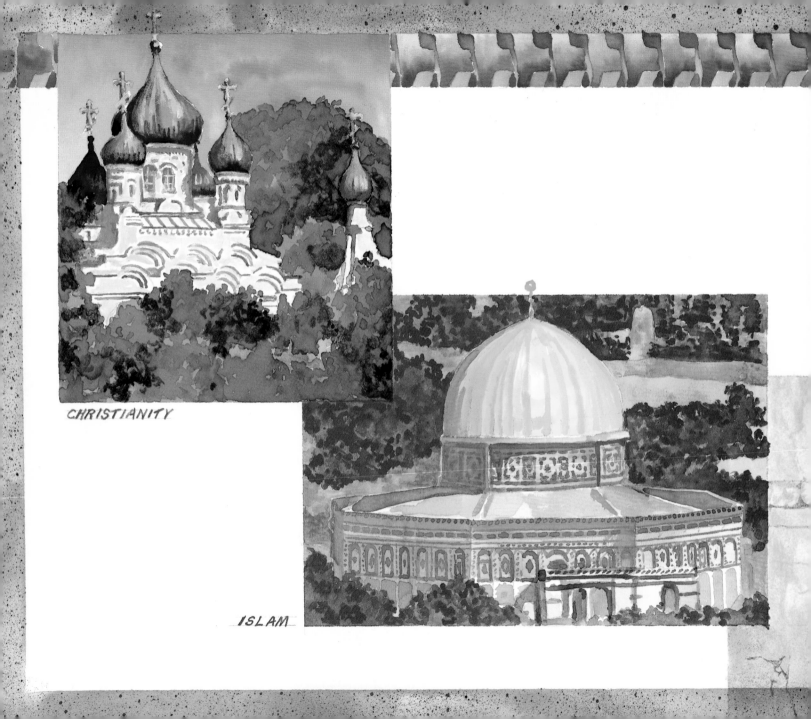

CHRISTIANITY

ISLAM

3

שָׁלֹשׁ **(shah-losh)**

    Israel, and especially its capital, Jerusalem, is a sacred place for **three** of the world's largest religions—Judaism, Christianity, and Islam. Two smaller religions, Baha'i and Druze, also have holy shrines in this country. Followers of all these religions live in Israel.

    Because so many religions have a historical and emotional attachment to the area of Israel, it has been called the Holy Land. People from all over the world come to visit Israel's sacred sites each year.

JUDAISM

ארבע (ar-bah)

An important holiday for the Jews of Israel, as well as of the world, is Passover. Every spring, families gather together for the Passover dinner, called the seder meal, and ask the **Four** Questions. The Four Questions, or *Arbah Sh'elot* (ar-ba-ah sh-ay-loat), help Jews to remember how in ancient times Moses led them from slavery in Egypt to freedom in the land of Israel.

The Four Questions are traditionally asked by children. The father or the leader of the seder meal answers them. Each question asks in various ways why this Passover meal is different from any other meal. The answers describe the bitterness of slavery, the haste of the Jews' flight from Egypt, the pain of being in the desert, and the joy of freedom.

SEDER PLATE

karpas (greens)

CANDLES

salt water

lamb bone

Elijah's cup

egg

maror (bitter herbs)

haroset (fruit and nuts)

MATZOH

GRAPE JUICE OR WINE

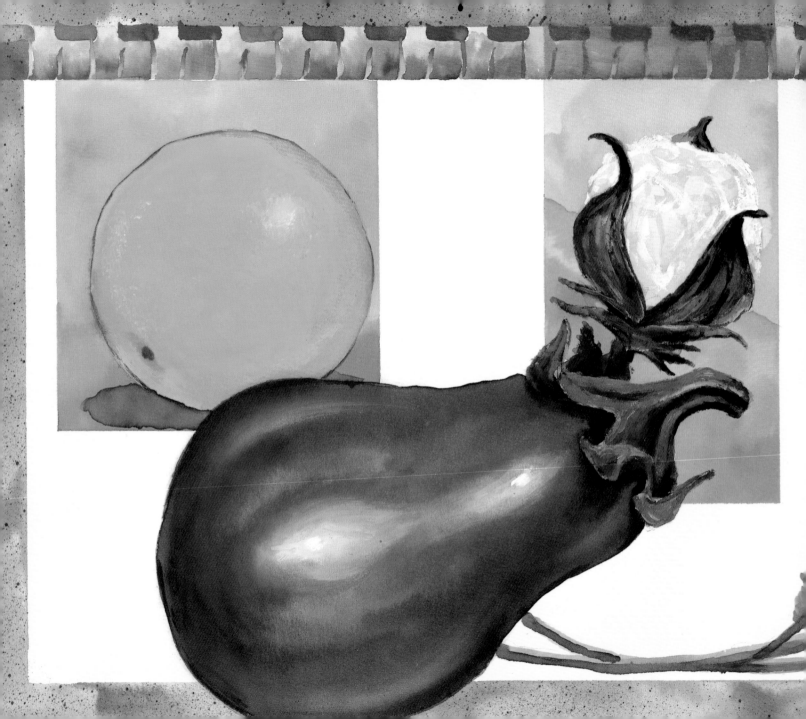

5

חמש (Hah-mesh)

Five agricultural products for which Israel is well known are citrus fruits, vegetables, nuts, cotton, and flowers. Before the State of Israel was founded in 1948, much of its land was barren desert. The land had been lived on and farmed for thousands of years, and it had been stripped of most of its plant life. Much of the soil had dried up, and nothing could be grown on it.

One of the biggest challenges for the new country was to grow its own food. In just over 40 years, Israel has irrigated large areas of its land and planted hundreds of millions of trees, making the soil productive once again. Now Israel is not only able to grow most of its own food, but it even exports crops to other countries.

 **(shaysh)**

Israel is a democratic republic, where all adult citizens, regardless of racial or religious background, have the right to vote. The majority of citizens are Jewish. The **six**-pointed Star of David, a traditional Jewish symbol, fills the center of the Israeli flag. The colors of the flag—blue and white—are the colors of the *tallit*, or Jewish prayer shawl. The tallit is a rectangular piece of cloth with tassels on all four corners that is worn by men at religious services.

ז

שבע (sheh-vah)

There are **seven** branches to a *menorah*, which is a Jewish candelabrum that has been important throughout Judaic history. Some people believe the menorah's seven branches stand for the seven days of creation written about in Judeo-Christian scriptures.

The menorah is the official symbol of Israel. A large carved monument of a menorah stands outside the *Knesset* building, which houses the Israeli legislature.

Menorahs are not the only Jewish candelabrum. For instance, a nine-branch candelabrum is used at *Hanukkah* (HAN-nu-ka), a Jewish festival of lights. This candelabrum is called a *hanukkiyyah* (Han-nu-KEE-yah).

ANDERSON SCHOOL
35W071 Villa Maria Rd.
St. Charles, IL 60174

שמונה (shmoh-neh)

Many animals that lived in the area of Israel during ancient times have disappeared, or nearly disappeared, in recent centuries. Through the efforts of the Israeli government, **eight** animals that can be found in Israel once more are the Judean Desert leopard, the ibex (a wild goat), the Mesopotamian fallow deer, the striped hyena, the hyrax, the Asiatic wild ass, the white oryx, and the ostrich.

Most of these animals were reintroduced to Israel by the Hai-Bar (a Hebrew term meaning "wildlife") Program. The program works to find "lost" animals in other parts of the world and bring them back to Israel. The animals are then carefully tended and eventually let loose to live freely in their natural habitats. The program has been successful.

Israel has strict rules that protect its animals, and all hunting is strictly forbidden. Over one fourth of the country is set aside in nature reserves or natural forest.

HYRAX

ORYX

OSTRICH

JUDEAN
DESERT
LEOPARD

ASIATIC
WILD ASS

IBEX

MESOPOTAMIAN
FALLOW
DEER

STRIPED HYENA

9

עשׂת (tay-shah)

Nine products that Israel exports to other parts of the world are polished diamonds, military equipment (such as fighter planes), x-ray machines, clothing, leather goods, computers, chemicals, solar-energy technology, and irrigation systems.

Some of these products are produced by a type of community called a *kibbutz* (kih-BOOTS), where people live and work together for the good of the community. A kibbutz can be set up for farming or for manufacturing. Kibbutz members receive no salaries, but in exchange for their work, the kibbutz pays for all their needs. Each kibbutz is run in a democratic way, with the people voting on matters that concern everyone.

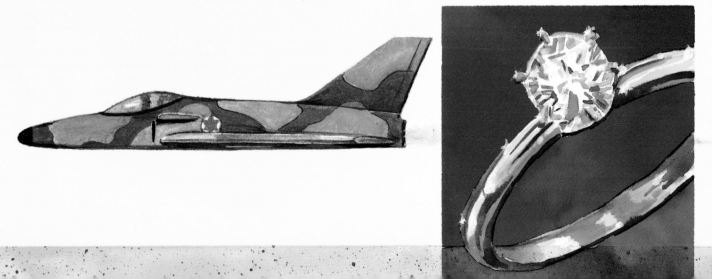

10

עֶשֶׂר **(e-sair)**

The Jewish people descended from twelve nomadic tribes who lived in ancient times in the area now known as Israel. About 3,000 years ago, **ten** of the tribes broke away from the original Kingdom of Israel. They formed a separate kingdom in the northern regions. The other two tribes, located to the south, formed a new kingdom called Judah. The word "Jew" comes from the name of that kingdom, but it describes the descendants of all the Israelite tribes.

About 200 years after the Kingdom of Israel split in two, the Assyrians (people from the area of present-day Iraq) conquered the northern kingdom. The ten conquered tribes became known as the Ten Lost Tribes because they were scattered to all parts of the world.

Over the centuries, the people of Judah were also dispersed to other parts of the world. But with the founding of the modern State of Israel, all Jews can make a home in this land once again.

Pronunciation Guide

1 / אחת (ah-Hat)

2 / שתים (shtah-yim)

3 / שלש (shah-losh)

4 / ארבע (ar-bah)

5 / חמש (Hah-maysh)

6 / שש (shaysh)

7 / שבע (sheh-vah)

8 / שמונה (shmoh-neh)

9 / תשע (tay-shah)

10 / עשר (e-sair)